Food . Faith . Family

Blessings!

[signature] 2019

simply southern

a southern legacy

"Then God said,
'I give you every seed-bearing
plant on the face of the whole
earth and every tree that
has fruit with seed in it.
They will be yours for food."

GENESIS 1:29

tina webb

simply southern

simple. good. food

"God created food to be received with Thanksgiving by those who believe and who know the truth... He richly provides us with everything for our enjoyment."

I TIMOTHY 4:3, 6:7

preface

As I prepared each dish for this book, I wanted to say that it was easy or simple, and that is why I titled this book *simply.southern*. Most of the recipes in this book have been handed down for generations. I am born and raised a southern Texas girl, and this is what I know best: God, family, friends and food.

I wanted to share my love and passion for food, and writing this book seemed like a perfect opportunity to do that. I have known for years that God had a special project for me, and I feel like this book is part of His plan for me.

One of the things I remember growing up was my mom and grandmother's cooking. It felt so good to visit my grandmother and enjoy all the things she prepared to eat. I would think to myself, "How can food taste so good?" My mom always cooked dinner, and I can't remember eating out very much. We all had gardens and everything was fresh. At holidays, the cookies, noodles, or meats were things you could not wait to dig in to. I have received the lineage of home-cooked meals and enjoy being in the kitchen, preparing dishes of love for family and friends. When I feel stressed, overwhelmed, or in need of a break, I actually like to bake or cook. Though not to label myself a connoisseur of food, I am at a place in my life where I like to enjoy good foods. I have so many tried and true recipes, made with fresh ingredients that are so tasty that they are hard to beat. We enjoy these recipes that have been around for years and even centuries, that it's hard not to share them.

It's no secret my husband, Brion, is from Maine. His mother, Marlene, is such a wonderful cook and has fabulous recipes that I had to include in this book. I know these recipes are not from the South, however, you would never know it. My Maine family is so sweet, hospitable, and just down-home good people. Marlene's recipes are family favorites too and have been passed down for generations. I know you will enjoy her simple and tasty recipes.

I hope that you find comfort and fun in preparing and sharing these recipes. Thank you for purchasing this cookbook, and I hope your family can create their own legacies of recipes for your generations to come!

So whether you eat or drink or whatever you do,
do it all for the glory of God.
1 Corinthians 10:31

ISBN 978-1-64258-070-9 (paperback)
ISBN 978-1-64258-071-6 (digital)
ISBN 978-1-64258-072-3 (hardback)

Front and Back covers by:
Uncle Tio Photography

Front cover: St. James Lutheran Church of
New Wehdem

Christian Faith Publishing, Inc.
832 Park Avenue
Meadville, PA 16335
www.christianfaithpublishing.com

Printed in the United States of America

a southern legacy

contents

roots

Though leaves fall
And branches break
The tree grows tall
And roots make their stake

We too may take a fall
And promises we break
Our faith grows tall
And God's word is our stake

The rain is engulfed by the ground
A spring of water it creates
The living water for the roots is found
The tree grows and its beauty abounds

God's word is poured into our mind
It is a spring of hope and love
For now our hearts are pure and kind
And glistening white and pure as doves

The roots of the tree
Stay strong with the living spring
We too have roots for all to see
God's living Word in us shall we cling.

Tina

supporting a cause

A portion of the sales of each cookbook will be donated to Adam's Angels Ministry

January, 2003, my friends Donna and Tim Culliver's lives were changed forever. Their son Adam, four years old, lost his life to Acute Myelogenous Leukemia. I remember talking to Donna when she told me that Adam was ill and she had taken him to the local clinic where they said he had the Norwalk virus. In the middle of the night, we got a call that Adam was being transferred to Texas Children's Hospital in Houston, that his blood count levels were extremely high. I went as soon as I could and just hugged Donna. The doctors soon diagnosed Adam with AML, Acute Myelogenous Leukemia. And just like that, all our lives would change forever.

Unless you've faced the challenges of having a child with cancer, it is almost impossible to comprehend the devastation families experience. Donna and Tim know the day-to-day realities of what families must learn to cope with from their own personal tragedy. The challenge of juggling emotional and spiritual pain, along with financial obligations, is overwhelming.

Adam's Angels Ministry was founded in 2004 out of deep understanding and compassion for families battling childhood cancer. The ministry provides care and comfort through physical, emotional, financial and spiritual support. All donations directly benefit patients and their families. No paid staff, all volunteer. For more information visit, AdamsAngelsMinistry.org

I have felt led to make a difference in someone's life. I can't think of a better organization to help children and families in need dealing with such tragic news that their child has cancer. I know Donna and Tim and their dedication to the Lord and I am excited to help them help others. Thank you for your purchase of this cookbook and for helping me support a worthy cause for many children and families.

"Praise be to God and the Father of our Lord Jesus Christ, the Father of compassion and the God of all comfort, who comforts us in all our troubles, so that we can comfort those in any trouble with the comfort that we ourselves have received from God."

II CORINTHIANS 1:3-5

Brion's Favorite

Oatmeal, Peanut Butter, & Chocolate Chunk Cookies

Well,
I DECLARE

Sunday Lunch

Roast Beef and Gravy

Mashed Potatoes

Green Bean Rolls

Rolls

Icebox Pickles

Sweet Iced Tea

Red Velvet Cake

Say yer
prayers
sunday lunch

fixin'
to

Serrano Pepper
Ranch Dressing

1 dry package Ranch Buttermilk Dressing
1 cup buttermilk
1 cup mayo
2 serrano peppers (for mild remove ribs and seeds)

Mix together in a small food chopper, then chill.

Texas Caviar

1 (14 oz.) can blackeye peas, drained
1 (14 oz.) can white hominy, drained
1 medium size tomato, chopped
4 green onions
2 garlic cloves
½ cup onion, chopped
1 ½ cups chunky picante sauce

Mix together and refrigerate.

Fresh Salsa

1 (28 oz.) can diced tomatoes
2 cans Ro-Tel (one mild and one regular)
¼ cup onion, diced
2 jalapenos (remove ribs and seeds for mild)
1 clove garlic, chopped
¼ teaspoon sugar
¼ teaspoon salt
¼ teaspoon cumin
1 bunch cilantro
Juice from ½ lime

Combine all ingredients in bowl. Pulse together in blender or small hand chopper, you may need to do in increments. Stir together once blended and add more salt if needed. Store in air tight container in refrigerator.

Cracker Dip

1 (3 oz.) can chopped black olives
1 onion, chopped
1 large tomato, chopped
1 (4 oz.) can green chilies

Mix together and then add seasoning:

1 ½ tablespoons vinegar
3 tablespoons oil
Garlic salt to taste

Mix well and chill for at least 2 hours before serving.

Chunky Fresh Salsa

8 roman tomatoes, diced
1 red onion, chopped
3 cloves garlic, chopped
4 lemons, juice
1 bunch cilantro, chopped
½ jar chunky picante sauce
Season to taste with Tony Chachere's seasoning and
salt (or any creole seasoning)

Mix together and refrigerate.

Edna's Shrimp Dip

1 pound boiled baby shrimp
1 cup mayo
1 (8 oz.) cream cheese
6 green onions, chopped
2 stalks celery, finely chopped
1 teaspoon Old Bay seafood seasoning

Mix and chill. Serve with crackers or chips.

Avocado Dip

4 avocados
1 (16 oz.) sour cream
1 (14.5 oz.) can Ro-Tel tomatoes
1 tablespoon garlic powder
1 (4 oz.) green chilies, chopped
2 teaspoons salt
1 teaspoon lemon juice
3 oz. cream cheese

Mix together in blender or food chopper and chill.

Raspberry Chipotle Dip

1 jar Fischer & Wieser Chipotle Sauce
1 large red onion, finely chopped
1 bunch cilantro, chopped
1 (11 oz.) can mandarin oranges, drained
1 (15.25 oz.) can corn, drained

Mix together and chill. Serve with chips or crackers.

Tomatillo Sauce

8 tomatillos
3 garlic cloves
3 jalapenos
¼ bunch cilantro

Put tomatillos, garlic and jalapenos in a 3 quart pot and add water just enough to cover. Boil until tomatillos are opened. Drain and put into blender adding cilantro.

IT'S *your*
Bread & Butter

My mother-in-law, Marlene, is an amazing cook.
She has shared many family recipes with me and taught me so much.
Her recipes are handed down from family traditions in Maine.

"They broke bread in their
homes and ate together
with glad and sincere hearts."
ACTS 2:46

Marlene's Biscuits

2 cups flour
3 teaspoons baking powder
Pinch of sugar
1 teaspoon salt
¼ cup shortening
¾ cup milk

Mix first five ingredients and then gradually add milk. Take out small amounts of dough and do not roll, slightly pat out dough on board to approximately ¾ inch thickness and cut out 2-3 inch circles for rolls. Place on slightly greased baking pan approximately ½ inch apart so rolls will touch as they bake. Bake at 450 degrees for 20 minutes or until golden brown.

Yield: 10-12

Pumpkin Bread

⅓ cup shortening
1 ⅓ cups sugar
½ teaspoon vanilla
2 eggs
⅓ cup water
1 ⅔ cups flour
½ teaspoon baking soda
1 teaspoon baking powder
½ teaspoon cinnamon
½ teaspoon nutmeg
¾ teaspoon salt
1 cup canned pumpkin
½ cup chopped pecans

Cream shortening and add sugar and vanilla. Add eggs one at a time, beating thoroughly after each addition. Gently mix in water. In separate bowl, thoroughly mix flour, baking soda, baking powder, cinnamon, nutmeg and salt. Add gradually to the shortening mixture and beat until smooth. Add pumpkin and mix gently. Set aside 3 tablespoons of chopped pecans and then fold remaining pecans into batter. Lightly grease and flour a loaf pan. Pour batter into loaf pan, and sprinkle with the remaining pecans on the top. Bake at 350 degrees for 45 to 50 minutes or until golden brown.

Marlene's Gingerbread

3 cups flour
1 teaspoon cinnamon
1 teaspoon ground ginger
1 teaspoon ground cloves
1 teaspoon baking soda
1 cup packed brown sugar
½ cup melted Crisco shortening
1 cup molasses
2 eggs
1 cup boiling water

Topping: powdered sugar and whipped cream (optional)

Mix together first five dry ingredients and set aside. Blend brown sugar and shortening, then add molasses and eggs, mixing well. Add dry ingredients to mixture and slowly fold in boiling water. Bake in 9x13 pan at 350 degrees for 25 minutes. Sprinkle with powdered sugar and top with whipped cream.

Golden Cornbread

1 cup corn meal
¼ cup sugar
4 teaspoons baking powder
1 cup flour
½ teaspoon salt
1 egg
1 cup milk
¼ cup butter flavor Crisco

Put dry ingredients together. Add egg, milk, and shortening. Mix till smooth.
Pour into a greased 8-inch baking pan. Bake at 425 degrees for 25 to 30 minutes.

Recipe doubled for larger 11 ¼ size cast iron skillet as shown in picture.

Sugah
& SPICE

Marlene's Chocolate Donuts

1 teaspoon baking soda
1 cup sour milk (combine 1 ½ teaspoons white vinegar in a cup and then fill remaining cup with milk)
3 cups flour
1 cup sugar
½ teaspoon salt
3 teaspoons baking powder
1 teaspoon cinnamon
2 eggs
2 tablespoons butter
1 ½ squares unsweetened chocolate, melted
1 ½ teaspoons vanilla

Cinnamon and sugar for topping: Mix 4 tablespoons sugar with 1 teaspoon cinnamon

Dissolve baking soda in 1 cup sour milk. Sift together flour, sugar, salt, baking powder, and cinnamon. Mix dry ingredients together with eggs, butter, chocolate and vanilla. Then add milk mixture. If dough seems too moist, add up to ½ cup more flour to thicken. Roll out dough to about ½ inch thickness and cut into donuts using donut cutter. Cook in hot oil until golden brown on both sides. Dust with sugar and cinnamon.

Yield: Approx. 24-30 depending on size of donut cutter

Marlene's White Donuts

1 cup sugar
2 eggs
1 teaspoon nutmeg
2 tablespoons Crisco oil
1 teaspoon salt
1 teaspoon baking soda

¼ teaspoon cream of tartar
1 cup buttermilk
1 teaspoon vanilla
3 ½ cups flour

Cinnamon and sugar for topping: Mix 4 tablespoons sugar to 1 teaspoon cinnamon

Combine all ingredients. If dough seems too moist, add up to ½ cup more flour to thicken.
Roll out dough to about ½ inch thickness and cut into donuts using donut cutter. Cook in
hot oil until golden brown on both sides. Dust with sugar and cinnamon.

Yield: Approx. 24-30 depending on size of donut cutter

Marlene's Molasses Donuts

½ **cup cold water**
½ **teaspoon coffee**
1 **cup molasses**
1 **egg**
½ **teaspoon salt**

½ **teaspoon cinnamon**
1 **tablespoon melted shortening**
½ **teaspoon baking soda**
3 **cups flour**

Cinnamon and sugar for topping: Mix 4 tablespoons sugar to 1 teaspoon cinnamon

Combine all ingredients. If dough seems too moist, add up to ½ cup more flour to thicken. Roll out dough to about ½ inch thickness and cut into donuts using donut cutter. Cook in hot oil until golden brown on both sides. Dust with sugar and cinnamon.

Yield: Approx. 24-30 depending on size of donut cutter

Edna's Pear Pie

4 cups peeled and sliced pears
½ cup sugar
3 tablespoons flour
½ teaspoon cinnamon
¼ teaspoon nutmeg
3 tablespoons pear juice
⅛ teaspoon lemon juice
1 pie crust

Grease and prepare pie dish with crust. Mix above ingredients and pour into prepared pie crust. Bake at 350 degrees for 20-30 minutes until lightly browned.

Edna was my former mother-in-law and she had a contagious zest for life! She taught me so many wonderful family recipes. I miss her dearly but the memories of these recipes make me smile every time I make them.

Marlene's Whoopie Pies

½ cup unsweetened dark cocoa powder
½ cup boiling water
½ cup shortening
1 ½ cups sugar
2 eggs
2 ¾ cups flour
1 teaspoon baking soda
1 teaspoon baking powder
½ teaspoon salt
1 teaspoon vanilla
½ cup sour milk (put 1½ teaspoons white vinegar in cup and add milk to make ½ cup)

Filling:
1 cup warm milk
5 tablespoons flour
Pinch of salt
1 cup sugar
½ cup shortening
½ cup softened butter
2 teaspoons vanilla

Mix ½ cup dark cocoa with ½ cup boiling water and set aside to cool. Cream shortening and sugar and then add eggs. Sift together flour, baking soda, baking powder, and salt. Add to cream mixture. Finally, add vanilla and sour milk. Drop by heaping tablespoons on greased cookie sheet. Put flour on your fingers to flatten a little. Bake at 350 degrees for 12 minutes. Allow cake to cool before adding filling.

For filling, mix milk, flour and salt over medium heat until it thickens. Remove from heat and allow to completely cool, stirring occasionally. While cooling combine sugar, shortening, butter, and vanilla. Once milk, flour and salt mixture is cooled, add remaining ingredients and whip until light and fluffy. You may need to whip several times to get fluffy.

Keep cool until serving. Yield: 16-18

This recipe can also be used as a cake. Place chocolate batter into 9x13 pan and bake at 350 degrees for 30 minutes or until toothpick inserted comes out clean. Allow to cool and spread filling over top of cake.

Dewberry Crunch

1 (20 oz.) can crushed pineapples
⅔ cup sugar
4 cups dewberries (or substitute for blackberries)
1 yellow box cake mix
3 tablespoons butter, melted
1 cup pecans, chopped
⅓ cup sugar

Layer ingredients in 9x13 greased dish, starting with can of pineapples and their juice. Sprinkle sugar on top of pineapples, then dewberries. Add the dry cake mix on top of the dewberries. Drizzle melted butter over top of dry cake mix. Sprinkle top of cake with pecans and remaining sugar. Bake at 350 degrees for 20 minutes. Remove cake and cut with spoon or knife all over cake to let the juices rise. Bake for another 20 minutes.

Bessie's Kolaches

Crust:
2 heaping teaspoons dry yeast
½ cup warm water

Mix and let dissolve for 5 minutes.

4 egg yolks
½ cup sugar
1 teaspoon salt
1 (5 oz.) can evaporated milk
⅔ cup oil
2 cups warm milk
6-7 cups flour

1 large egg white, beaten

Fruit Filling:
Use one 18 oz. jar of any kind of preserves. Warm in a pan with ⅓ cup of Minute tapioca.
Make one day ahead and refrigerate to allow filling to jell. Freeze any leftovers.

Cream Cheese Filling: Make one day ahead and refrigerate to allow filling to jell. Freeze any
leftovers. Mix together the follow:

1 (16 oz.) cottage cheese
2 (8 oz.) cream cheese
3 egg yolks
1 cup of sugar
⅓ cup Minute tapioca
2 tablespoons flour

Topping:
1 cup margarine
1 cup sugar
1 cup flour

Mix all ingredients for crust and knead well and then let rest about 10 minutes, and then
re-knead until smooth. Cover and let rise until double in size. Form approximately 1 ½ inch balls
(dust with flour to prevent sticking), place on cookie sheet and press indention in center. Add
fruit or cream cheese filling, using 1-2 teaspoons per kolache. Allow kolaches to rise. Sprinkle
with topping. Brush dough with egg white. Bake at 350 degrees for 25-30 minutes or until
lightly golden brown. Yield: 5 dozen

Pies, Pastries and Desserts

Growing up as little girl, I always loved eating
Bessie's kolaches at my Grandma Broz's house. My
grandmother is no longer living, but Bessie is and she
is 95 years old. Bessie had a close relationship with my
grandmother and they were related by marriage. She
is a living icon of all women living almost 100 years ago.
I marvel at her zest for life and the way she still loves
to bake for those she loves. This recipe is a true legacy
handed down for many generations.

Mom's Mini Pecan Pies

Crust:

1 cup sifted flour
1 stick butter
1 (8 oz.) cream cheese, softened

Filling:

¾ cup brown sugar
1 egg
½ teaspoon vanilla
1 tablespoon melted butter
⅔ cup pecans, chopped

Combine crust ingredients together and chill dough for 30 minutes. Grease cupcake pan and press crust dough on bottom and half way up each mold. Combine filling ingredients and use a teaspoon and fill prepared crust molds. Bake at 325 degrees for 25 minutes or until lightly browned. Allow to cool before removing from molds.

Yield: 24 pies

Banana Nut Muffins

2 ¼ cups all-purpose flour
3 teaspoons baking powder
½ teaspoon salt
½ teaspoon cinnamon
4 overripe bananas
1 ½ cups sugar
¾ cup soft unsalted butter
2 eggs
1 teaspoon vanilla
½ cup pecans, chopped

Preheat oven to 375 degrees and lightly grease and flour 24 muffin pans or use liners. In a large bowl, combine the flour, baking powder, cinnamon and salt; set aside. With an electric mixer, whip the bananas and sugar together for a good 3 minutes. Add the soft butter, eggs and vanilla and beat well scraping down the sides of the bowl once or twice. Mix in the dry ingredients. Fold in the pecans. Spoon batter into the muffin pans to fill them about halfway. Bake about 20 minutes or until toothpick comes out clean. Let cool a few minutes before removing.

Yield: 24 muffins

Edna's Dewberry Pie

1 ½ cups sugar
½ cup flour
Pinch of salt
2 well beaten eggs
½ cup sour cream
4 cups dewberries (can substitute
blackberries)
1 pie crust

Topping:

8 tablespoons flour
8 tablespoons sugar
4 tablespoons butter

Grease and prepare pie dish with
crust. Place dewberries into prepared
crust. Mix sugar, flour, salt, eggs and
sour cream. Pour mixture onto top of
dewberries and allow to settle. Mix
together topping ingredients and
sprinkle on top of dewberries. Bake
at 350 degrees for 45 minutes or until
golden brown.

gimme some SUGAR

"gracious words are a honeycomb, sweet to the soul and healing to the bones."

PROVERBS 16:24

Carrot cake recipe on Page 57

" Jesus said to them,
'I am the bread of life;
whoever comes to me
shall not hunger,
and whoever believes
in me shall never thirst."

JOHN 6:35

Cakes, Cookies and Candy

Carrot Cake

3 eggs
¾ cup of buttermilk
¾ cup vegetable oil
1 ½ cups white sugar
2 teaspoon vanilla extract
¼ teaspoon salt
2 teaspoons ground cinnamon

2 cups all-purpose flour
2 teaspoons baking soda
2 cups shredded carrots
1 cup flaked coconut
1 (8 oz.) can crushed pineapples with juice
1 cup chopped walnuts

Preheat oven to 350 degrees. Grease and flour three 8-inch cake round pans. Combine eggs, buttermilk, oil, sugar and vanilla, mix well. Add in flour, baking soda, salt and cinnamon. Mix until well blended. Next add carrots, coconut, crushed pineapples with juice and chopped walnuts. Mix until blended. Pour into prepared pans and bake at 350 degrees for 35 minutes. Allow to cool in cake pans. Remove from pans and onto cake plate to frost each layer.

Cream Cheese Frosting

½ cup butter (softened)
1 (8 oz.) cream cheese (softened)

1 teaspoon vanilla extract
1-pound powdered sugar

Beat the butter and cream cheese until fluffy. Add in the vanilla and sifted powdered sugar and beat until smooth. If the frosting is too thin add powdered sugar 2 tablespoons at a time and if too thick add a teaspoon of milk at a time.

Cakes, Cookies and Candy

Grandma Broz's
Macaroon Kisses

2 egg whites
¼ cup sugar
¼ teaspoon cream of tartar
¼ teaspoon salt
½ teaspoon vanilla
1 cup coconut
2 cups frosted corn flakes

Beat egg whites until stiff. Gradually add sugar, cream of tartar, salt and vanilla, beat stiff. Then fold in coconut and frosted corn flakes. Grease and lightly flour cookie sheet. Bake at 325 degrees for approximately 20 minutes or until golden brown. Remove from pan right away.

Yield: 12 cookies

Grandma Broz's Pineapple Coffee Cake

Cake:

1 ½ cups sugar
½ teaspoon salt
2 beaten eggs
1 teaspoon baking soda
2 cups crushed pineapples with juice
2 cups flour
⅓ cup oil
½ teaspoon vanilla

Topping:

1 cup flour
1 cup sugar
1 stick softened butter

Mix above cake ingredients together and pour into two 8x8 or one 9x13 greased and floured pans. Mix topping ingredients and sprinkle on top of cake mixture. Bake at 325 degrees for 30 minutes or until done.

Chocolate Cheesecake

Crust:
1 cup crushed chocolate cookies (I use chocolate teddy graham cookies)
3 tablespoons sugar
3 tablespoons melted butter

Mix together and press on bottom of greased 9" spring-form pan and set aside.

Filling:
12 oz. semi-sweet chocolate chips
2 (8 oz.) cream cheese
¾ cup sugar
2 eggs
1 teaspoon vanilla
2 tablespoons flour

Melt chocolate chips and set aside. Beat together cream cheese, sugar, eggs, vanilla and flour. Fold in melted chocolate. Pour into prepared crust. Bake at 350 degrees for 40-45 minutes until set. Turn oven off and allow cheesecake to cool in oven, this will prevent the cheesecake from falling.

Cheesecake

Crust:
2 ½ cups graham cracker crumbs
⅓ cup sugar
½ teaspoon cinnamon
½ cup melted butter

Filling:
3 (8 oz.) packages softened cream cheese
1 ½ cups sugar
1 teaspoon vanilla
4 eggs, separated

Topping:
½ cup sour cream
2 tablespoons sugar
½ teaspoon vanilla
½ cup cool whip

Combine cracker crumbs, sugar and cinnamon. Stir in butter. Press onto bottom and 2 inches up sides of greased 9" spring-form pan. Bake at 350 degrees for 5 minutes. Cool.

Reduce heat in oven to 325 degrees.

Beat cream cheese, sugar and vanilla. Add egg yolks, beat slowly until mixed. Beat egg whites until stiff and fold into cream cheese mixture. Pour over crust. Bake 1 hour or until center is almost set. Turn oven off and leave in oven until cooled, this will prevent it from falling. Refrigerate for about an hour until completely cooled.

Combine sour cream, sugar and vanilla. Fold in cool whip. Spread over cheesecake. Refrigerate overnight. Remove sides of pan and bottom very carefully. Leave bottom on.

Grandma Broz's Sugar Cookies

¾ cup shortening
2 cups sugar
2 eggs
¼ cup milk
1 teaspoon vanilla

4 cups flour
¼ teaspoon nutmeg
3 teaspoons baking powder
Topping: Candied sprinkles

Mix together one cup of sugar with shortening, then add one egg and mix. Add another cup sugar to mixture and then the remaining egg. Then add milk and vanilla. Add 2 cups flour to mixture, then nutmeg and baking powder, once mixed then add remaining 2 cups flour. Chill dough for 45-60 minutes. Roll out dough on prepared surface approx. ¼ inch (thin) and use cookie cutters for shapes. Top with candied sprinkles. Bake at 350 degrees for 8-10 minutes on greased cookie sheet.

Yield: Approximately 4 dozen

My mom, Peggy, continues the tradition of family recipes handed down from my Grandma Broz. We are making one of our favorites, Grandma Broz's sugar cookies. The legacy continues with each generation as we learn these recipes and pass along to our children. I love creating a southern legacy through baking and cooking these great recipes.

Sugar Cookies

3/4 cup shortening
2 cup sugar
1/4 cup milk
2 egg's
1/4 tsp nutmeg
1 tsp Vanilla
3 tsp baking powder
4 cups flour
Roll out & cut out in shape's Bake 350°F

merry everything

Edna's Mandarin Orange Cake

1 package yellow butter cake mix
4 eggs
1 (11 oz.) can mandarin oranges, undrained
1 teaspoon vanilla
¾ cup Crisco oil

Topping:

1 (8 oz.) cool whip
1 (3 oz.) box instant vanilla pudding
1 (20 oz.) can crushed pineapples, undrained

Hand mix the cake ingredients using all the juice from the oranges. Bake in a 9x13 greased and floured pan at 350 degrees for 30 minutes or until toothpick inserted comes out clean. Let cool. Mix together topping using all the juice from the pineapples, and spread over cake, keep refrigerated.

Marlene's Molasses Cookies

3 ½ cups flour
¾ teaspoon salt
2 ½ teaspoons baking soda
1 teaspoon ground cinnamon
1 teaspoon ground ginger
½ teaspoon ground cloves
½ cup sugar
½ cup Crisco shortening
1 egg
⅔ cup sour milk (to make sour milk, put 2 teaspoons white vinegar in measuring cup and then add milk to make ⅔ cup)
1 cup molasses

Mix first six dry ingredients and set aside. Cream sugar and shortening, add egg, sour milk and molasses. Add dry ingredients and stir. Drop by spoonful onto greased cookie sheet and put flour on your fingers to flatten a little. Bake at 350 degrees for 10-12 minutes.

Yield: Approx. 30 cookies

Soft Chocolate Chip Cookies

4 ½ cups all-purpose flour
2 teaspoons baking soda
2 cups butter, softened
1 ½ cups packed brown sugar
½ cup white sugar
2 (3.4 oz.) packages instant vanilla pudding mix
4 eggs
2 teaspoons vanilla extract
4 cups semi-sweet chocolate chips
2 cups chopped nuts (optional)

Sift together the flour and baking soda, set aside. In a large bowl, cream together the butter, brown sugar, and white sugar. Beat in the instant pudding mix until blended. Stir in the eggs and vanilla. Blend in the flour mixture. Finally, stir in the chocolate chips. Drop cookies by rounded spoonful onto ungreased cookie sheets.

Bake at 350 degrees for 10-12 minutes.

Yield: 4 dozen

Marlene's Sugar Cookies

1 ¼ cups sugar
½ cup unsalted butter
1 egg
½ cup sour milk (to make sour milk
put 1 ½ teaspoons white vinegar in
measuring cup and then add milk to
make ½ cup)
½ teaspoon salt
1 teaspoon vanilla
½ teaspoon baking soda
3 ¼ cups flour

Topping: Sugar or chocolate chips (optional)

Cream sugar and butter, add egg
and sour milk. Add dry ingredients,
vanilla and stir. Drop by spoonful onto
greased cookie sheet and put flour on
your fingers to flatten a little. Top with
sugar or chocolate chips. Bake at 350
degrees for 10-12 minutes.

Yield: 2 dozen

Texas Treat

6 cups Rice Chex
3 cups Cheerios
2 cups pretzels
1 cup peanuts
1 medium size bag of candy (candy corn or mini M&M's)
1 (20 oz.) white almond bark

Melt white almond bark and mix together with ingredients. Grease a couple of cookie sheets and pour mixture onto cookie sheets. Let cool in refrigerator for about 30 minutes to an hour. Break apart by pieces and store in air tight containers.

Edna's Chocolate Nutcake

1 stick butter
1 cup water
4 tablespoons unsweetened cocoa powder
1 teaspoon baking soda
2 beaten eggs
2 cups flour
½ cup buttermilk
2 cups sugar

Icing:

1 stick butter
4 tablespoons unsweetened cocoa powder
6 tablespoons milk
1 box powdered sugar
1 teaspoon vanilla
¾ cup pecans, chopped

Bring to boil 1 stick butter, add cocoa and 1 cup water. Mix 1 teaspoon baking soda in ½ cup buttermilk and let sit for 5 minutes. Then add to cocoa mixture. Continue and add 2 beaten eggs, sugar and flour. Stir well. Grease and flour 9x13 pan. Bake at 400 degrees for 25 minutes. While cake is in oven, prepare icing. Boil 1 stick butter, 4 tablespoons cocoa and 6 tablespoons milk. Remove and add 1 box powdered sugar, 1 teaspoon vanilla and ¾ cup chopped pecans. Pour icing over hot cake.

Chocolate Cake with Buttercream Frosting

Cake
2 cups all-purpose flour
2 cups sugar
¾ cup unsweetened cocoa powder
2 teaspoons baking powder
1 ½ teaspoons baking soda
1 teaspoon salt

1 cup milk
1 teaspoon espresso powder
½ cup vegetable oil
2 eggs
2 teaspoons vanilla extract
1 cup boiling water

Preheat oven to 350 degrees. Prepare two 9-inch cake pans with baking spray and lightly flour.

Add flour, sugar, cocoa, baking powder, baking soda, salt and espresso powder into a large bowl. Whisk through to combine well.

Add milk, oil, eggs, and vanilla to flour mixture and mix together on medium speed until well combined. Reduce speed and carefully add boiling water to the cake batter. Beat on high speed for about 1 minute to add air to the batter.

Distribute cake batter evenly between the two prepared cake pans. Bake for 30-35 minutes, or a toothpick comes out clean. Remove from oven and allow to cool for about 10 minutes, remove from pan and cool completely.

Chocolate Buttercream Frosting:
1 ½ cups butter (3 sticks), softened
1 cup unsweetened cocoa powder
5 cups confectioners sugar

½ cup milk
2 teaspoons vanilla extract
½ teaspoon espresso powder

Add cocoa to large bowl, whisk through to remove any lumps. Cream together butter and cocoa powder until well-combined.

Add sugar and milk to cocoa mixture by adding 1 cup of sugar followed by about a tablespoon of milk. After each addition has been combined, turn mixer onto a high speed for about a minute. Repeat until all sugar and milk have been added.

Add vanilla extract and espresso powder and combine well. If frosting appears too dry, add more milk, a tablespoon at a time until reaches the right consistency. If is appears too wet and does not hold its form, add more confectioners sugar, a tablespoon at a time until it reaches the right consistency. Refrigerate until serving.

Pumpkin Snickerdoodles

2 cups all-purpose flour
½ teaspoon baking soda
½ teaspoon cream of tartar
½ teaspoon salt
Pinch of ground nutmeg
1 stick unsalted butter, melted and cooled
1 cup sugar
½ cup canned pumpkin
1 large egg, room temperature
1 teaspoon vanilla
½ cup sanding sugar
1 teaspoon ground cinnamon
½ teaspoon ground allspice

Preheat oven to 375 degrees. In a medium bowl, whisk together flour, baking soda, cream of tartar, salt and nutmeg. In a large bowl, whisk together butter, sugar and pumpkin until smooth. Add egg and vanilla and whisk together to combine. Add flour mixture and stir to combine, about 2 minutes. In a small bowl, whisk together sanding sugar, cinnamon, and allspice.

Drop heaping tablespoons of dough into sugar mixture and roll into 1 ½ inch balls. Transfer to parchment-line rimmed baking sheets, 3 inches apart. Using a spatula, flatten balls to just under ½ inch thick. Sprinkle with more sugar mixture. Bake until golden brown 10-12 minutes. Let cool 5 minutes on sheets then transfer to wire rack.

Yield: 2 ½ dozen

Sour Cream Coffee Cake

1 box butter cake mix
¾ cup oil
½ cup sugar
4 eggs
1 cup sour cream
1 teaspoon vanilla
2 teaspoons cinnamon with 2 tablespoons sugar

Mix together cake mix, oil and sugar and beat. Add eggs, beating after each. Stir in sour cream with spoon. Add vanilla. Pour ½ of batter into a greased and floured Bundt pan.

Sprinkle with the cinnamon and sugar mixture. Pour remaining batter in pan. Bake at 350 degrees for 50-60 minutes.

Red Velvet Cake

2 cups all-purpose flour
1 teaspoon baking soda
1 teaspoon baking powder
1 teaspoon salt
2 tablespoons unsweetened cocoa powder
2 cups sugar
1 cup canola or vegetable oil

2 eggs
1 cup buttermilk
2 teaspoons vanilla extract
1-2 oz. red food coloring
1 teaspoon white vinegar
½ cup of prepared plain hot coffee

Preheat oven to 325 degrees.

In a medium bowl, whisk together flour, baking soda, baking powder, cocoa powder and salt. Set aside.

In a large bowl, combine the sugar and oil. Mix in the eggs, buttermilk, vanilla and red food coloring until combined. Stir in the coffee and white vinegar. Combine the wet ingredients with the dry ingredients a little at a time, mixing after each addition, just until combined.

Generously grease and flour two round, 9 inch cake pans. Pour the batter evenly into each pan. Bake for 30-40 minutes or until toothpick inserted comes out clean. Let pans cool on a cooling rack until they are warm to the touch. Slide a knife around the inside of the pans to loosen the cake from the pan. Remove the cakes from the pan and let them cool. Frost the cake with cream cheese frosting.

Cream Cheese Frosting:
2 (8 oz.) cream cheese, softened
¼ cup milk
1 stick butter, softened

2 teaspoons vanilla extract
4 cups powdered sugar
Topping: ¼ cup chopped pecans

Add softened cream cheese into large bowl. Pour in milk, butter and vanilla. Mix until well combined. Pour in half of the powdered sugar. Mix until combined. Add the remaining powdered sugar. Mix until smooth and fluffy.

Use more milk if frosting is too thick and add more powdered sugar if too thin.

Marlene's Blueberry Crumb Cake

¼ **cup sugar**
2 **cups flour**
½ **teaspoon salt**
4 **teaspoons baking powder**
1 **egg**
2 **tablespoons melted shortening**
1 **cup milk**
1 **cup blueberries**

Topping:

½ **cup brown sugar**
½ **cup flour**
⅛ **teaspoon salt**
½ **teaspoon cinnamon**
2 **tablespoons melted shortening**

Sift first 4 cake ingredients. Add egg, milk and shortening, stirring well. Fold in blueberries. Pour into an 7.5x11 greased and floured pan. Mix topping ingredients and sprinkle on top. Bake at 375 degrees for 25-30 minutes or until toothpick inserted comes out clean.

Pumpkin Cupcakes with Cinnamon and Honey Glaze

1 cup whole wheat flour
1 cup all-purpose flour
1 ½ cups sugar
2 teaspoons baking powder
½ teaspoon baking soda
½ teaspoon pumpkin pie spice
½ teaspoon salt
1 medium size sweet potato, baked, skin removed

1 ½ cups sugar
1 stick butter, softened
3 eggs
½ cup milk
1 (15 oz.) can pumpkin

Cinnamon Honey Glaze

¼ cup butter, melted
2 cups powdered sugar
2 tablespoons milk

½ teaspoon cinnamon
1 tablespoon honey

Preheat oven to 350 degrees. Coat a muffin pan with nonstick spray or cupcake liners. Combine all dry ingredients except sugar in a large mixing bowl, stir until just combined. Set aside.

In a separate bowl combine sugar and butter, and mix on medium speed until light and fluffy. Add eggs one at a time, incorporating completely each time.

In a third bowl, mash sweet potato with milk and pumpkin. Add ⅓ of dry ingredients to butter mixture and mix well. Add ⅓ of pumpkin mixture and combine well. Repeat until all ingredients are used.

Fill each muffin cup ½ to ¾ full. Bake for 25 minutes or until toothpick comes out clean. Cool completely on wire rack.

Glaze: Combine all ingredients until smooth. Drizzle top of each cupcake.

Oatmeal, Peanut Butter, Chocolate Chunk Cookies

1 cup flour
1 cup old fashioned oats
½ teaspoon baking powder
½ teaspoon baking soda
¼ teaspoon salt
½ cup butter, softened
½ cup sugar
½ cup packed brown sugar
½ cup creamy peanut butter
1 egg
1 ½ teaspoons vanilla
1 cup chocolate chunks

Heat oven to 375 degrees. Mix first 5 ingredients until blended. Beat butter, sugars and peanut butter in large bowl with mixer until light and fluffy. Add egg and vanilla; mix well. Gradually add flour mixture, mixing well after each addition. Stir in chocolate. Drop heaping tablespoons of dough, 2 inches apart, onto baking sheets. Bake 10 to 12 minutes or until lightly browned. Cool 1 minute on baking sheet; remove to wire racks. Cool completely.

TAKE YOUR OWN
Sweet Time

"Blessed are those who
hunger and thirst for
righteousness,
for they will be filled."
MATTHEW 5:6

Hearty Potato Soup

6 medium potatoes, peeled and sliced
2 carrots, diced
2 celery stalks, diced
1 onion, chopped
1 stick of butter

6 tablespoons flour
1 teaspoon salt
½ teaspoon pepper
1 ½ cups milk

In large pot, cook potatoes, carrots, and celery in water until tender for about 20 minutes. Drain, reserving liquid and setting vegetables aside. In same pot, saute onion in butter until tender; stir in flour, salt and pepper. Gradually add milk, stirring constantly until thickened; gently stir in vegetables. Add 1 cup (or more) of reserved liquid until soup is desired consistency. Add more salt and pepper to taste.

Yield: 8-12 servings

Grandma Broz's Homemade Chili

4 pounds chili meat
1 ½ teaspoons salt
1 tablespoon chili powder
1 (8 oz.) can tomato sauce
1 tablespoon Worcestershire sauce
2 onions, chopped
2 tablespoons package chili seasoning
1 clove garlic, chopped
4 tablespoons paprika

Combine all ingredients and add water to desired consistency. Bring to boil, then reduce heat. Simmer, partially covered until meat is tender and chili has thickened, about an hour.

Edna's Seafood Gumbo

⅔ cup oil or bacon drippings
1 cup flour
3 large onions, chopped
3 ribs celery, chopped
5 cloves garlic, chopped
¼ bell pepper, chopped
2 quarts water
3 bay leaves
Tabasco to taste
Salt and pepper
1 teaspoon Worcestershire sauce
2 to 3 pounds okra
2 (8 oz.) cans tomato sauce
1 dozen raw crabs
1 bunch green onions, chopped
1 small bunch parsley, chopped
2 pounds raw shrimp
1-2 pounds crab meat
Oysters (optional)
1 tablespoon Gumbo filé

In skillet make roux with oil and flour. Cook until chocolate brown color. Be patient, it takes a little while. Add chopped vegetables and stir until wilted. Transfer to gumbo pot (not iron). Add water and boil. Add seasonings, okra and tomato sauce, simmer for 1 hour. Add crabs, green onions and parsley, boil for 20 minutes. Add shrimp 2-3 minutes after crabs. Just before serving add crab meat, oysters and Gumbo filé. Serve over rice.

Turkey Chili with Cannellini Beans

8 Hatch, Anaheim or Poblano chili peppers, fire roasted
¼ bunch cilantro, chopped
¼ cup olive oil
1 large onion, diced
4 cloves garlic, minced
2 teaspoons salt
3 pounds ground turkey

¼ cup all-purpose flour
¼ cup chili powder
3 tablespoons ground cumin
½ teaspoon pepper
Pinch of cayenne pepper
4 cups chicken stock
2 (15 oz.) cans cannellini beans, with liquid

In a blender, puree the roasted chilies and cilantro until smooth. Set aside.

Combine olive oil, onion, garlic and salt in a pot or deep skillet over medium-high heat. Cook until onion is translucent, 5 to 6 minutes. Add the turkey and cook until browned and cooked through, breaking it up with a wooden spoon, 7 to 8 minutes. Add the flour, chili powder, cumin, black pepper and cayenne and cook about 2 minutes. Deglaze the pot by adding the chicken stock and scraping up the browned bits from the bottom of the pot. Add the reserved pureed chilies and cilantro. Bring to a boil, then reduce heat to a low simmer. Add the beans and simmer, partially covered, until the turkey is tender and the chili has thickened, about 1 hour.

You can substitute ground beef for ground turkey. I cook in crock pot on low for 3 to 4 hours.

How to Fire-roast Chilies:

Place the chilies on a broiler pan or BBQ grill. Broil, turning until charred, about 2 minutes per side. Place in a bowl, cover with plastic wrap and let stand 4 minutes. Uncover and scrape away the charred skin, then cut the peppers in half and remove and discard the seeds, stems and membranes.

Chicken Noodle Soup

1 Whole Chicken
2 quarts water
½ onion, chopped
2 stalks celery, chopped
2 carrots, diced
3-5 chicken bouillon cubes
Salt and pepper to taste

1 (16 oz.) bag noodles of choice
Picture shown with Grandma Broz's homemade noodles

Bring one whole chicken in 2 quarts water to boil, add onion, celery, carrots, salt and pepper. Lower heat and simmer for an hour. I put in a crock pot for 2-3 hours. Remove chicken and debone, cutting into bite size pieces. Strain vegetables, reserving chicken stock.   Put chicken stock in a large pot and add
approximately 1 quart water, chicken bouillon cubes and bring to a boil. Add noodles until firm, about 10 minutes.

Remove from heat and add chicken and vegetables.

WELL,
I'll Be

"So whether you eat or drink
or whatever you do,
do it all for the glory of God."
I CORINTHIANS 10:31

Edna's Pea Salad

2 cans English peas, drained
2 cans French style beans, drained
¾ cup chopped celery

¾ cup chopped green onions
Small jar chopped pimentos

Bring to boil:
1 cup oil
½ cup apple cider vinegar
1 cup sugar
1 teaspoon salt

Mix together and refrigerate overnight.

Wild Rice
and Chicken Salad

1 (14.5 oz.) can chicken broth
1 (6 oz.) box of long-grain and wild rice mix
2 cups shredded cooked chicken
2 celery ribs, thinly sliced
1 green bell pepper, chopped
1 small purple onion, chopped
Lemon-Mustard Dressing or dressing of your choice

Bring chicken broth to a boil and stir in rice mix and seasoning packet. Return to boil; cover and reduce heat and simmer 30 minutes or until rice is tender. Cool. Stir together rice mixture, chicken, and remaining ingredients. Chill at least 30 minutes.

Lemon-Mustard Dressing:
¼ cup olive oil
2 tablespoons water
2 teaspoons red wine vinegar
2 teaspoons lemon juice
2 teaspoons Dijon mustard
1 teaspoon minced garlic
⅛ teaspoon pepper
¼ teaspoon salt
Fresh herbs

Mix together and add desired amount to salad.

Edna's
Pistachio Pudding Salad

1 large can crushed pineapples, not drained
1 (12 oz.) cool whip
1 (3.4 oz.) box pistachio instant pudding
1 cup miniature marshmallows
1 cup chopped pecans

Mix together and refrigerate.

Marinated Tomatoes

Layer in Bowl:
Sliced tomatoes
Very thinly sliced onions

Sprinkle each layer:
Salt and pepper
Dry basil
1 teaspoon vinegar
½ teaspoon sugar
1 teaspoon vegetable oil

Refrigerate.

Copper Pennies

1 (10.75 oz.) can tomato soup
½ cup oil
1 cup sugar
¾ cup vinegar
1 teaspoon salt
1 teaspoon pepper
1 teaspoon prepared mustard
1 teaspoon Worcestershire sauce

Put all in quart container and shake.

5 cups or more cooked, sliced carrots
1 medium onion, chopped
1 medium green pepper, diced

Mix together. Keep refrigerated 12 hours before serving. Keeps for 2 weeks.

Ramen Noodle Salad

2 packages beef Ramen noodles, uncooked, broken into small pieces
2 bunches green onions, chopped
1 cup slivered almonds
1 cup sunflower seeds
16 oz. shredded cabbage for slaw

Combine above ingredients in a large bowl. Pour dressing over and mix.

Dressing:

2 envelopes beef Ramen seasoning mix from Ramen noodle package
⅓ cup vinegar
1 cup vegetable oil
½ cup sugar

Refrigerate and allow at least 1 hour before serving.

Pasta Salad

1 (7 oz.) package LaBella Rosa Fideo Cortudo noodles
1 bunch finely chopped broccoli
3 tablespoons corn
1 can fine chopped black olives
Italian dressing – add enough to your liking
Cracked pepper
Nuts & sunflower seeds (optional)

Combine and refrigerate.

Green Bean Rolls

1 pound bacon
2 (14.5 oz.) cans cut green beans
1 ½ cups sugar
¾ cup butter
1 tablespoon garlic salt

Cut bacon in half and roll 3 to 4 green beans in each half slice bacon piece. Place rolls in small casserole dish. Mix sugar, butter and garlic salt in small saucepan over low heat until combined. Pour over green bean rolls. Bake uncovered in oven at 350 degrees for 30 minutes. Bake 45 minutes for crispier bacon.

Edna's Cranberry Salad

1 (12 oz.) package fresh cranberries
1 ½ cups sugar
2 tablespoons gelatin
½ cup orange juice
1 cup celery, chopped
1 cup unpeeled apples, chopped
1 cup pecans, chopped

Dissolve gelatin in orange juice over low heat. Boil cranberries in 2 cups water boiling until cranberries open. Mix with sugar, let stand for 15minutes. Then mix remaining ingredients and refrigerate overnight.

Edna's Cranberry Pineapple Salad

1 (12 oz.) package fresh cranberries
2 cups sugar
2 (3.4 oz.) instant strawberry Jell-O
1 (8 oz.) can crushed pineapples, drained
1 cup pecans, chopped

Boil cranberries in 2 cups waters until cranberries open, add sugar and continue to boil until combined. Add remaining ingredients and refrigerate overnight.

Broccoli Salad

Combine:

1 (3 oz.) cream cheese, softened
2 tablespoons vinegar
2 tablespoons sugar
2 tablespoons oil
1 tablespoon mustard
¼ teaspoon salt
⅛ teaspoon garlic salt

Add:

6 cups chopped broccoli
⅓ cups raisins
2 tablespoons chopped onion
Topping: ½ cup chopped pecans

Refrigerate and add chopped pecans on top before serving.

Spicy Sesame Noodle, Green Bean and Carrot Salad

¼ cup fresh lime juice
3 tablespoons canola oil
3 tablespoons soy sauce
2 tablespoons dark brown sugar
1 tablespoon oriental sesame oil
1 tablespoon minced garlic
1 tablespoon grated orange peel
2 small serrano chilies, stemmed, thinly sliced and into rounds

9 oz. green beans, trimmed, cut diagonally into ½ inch pieces

1 (9 oz.) package linguine

2 cups shredded peeled carrots
1 cup thinly sliced green onions

Stir first 8 ingredients in medium bowl to blend. Season dressing with salt and pepper. Let stand 30 minutes to blend flavors. Cook green beans in large pot of boiling salted water until crisp-tender, about 2 minutes. Transfer beans to cold water to cool. Drain well and pat dry with paper towels. Return water to boil. Add pasta and cook until just tender but still firm to bite. Drain and rinse pasta under cold water. Drain well. Combine green beans, pasta, carrots, green onions and dressing in large bowl. Toss to coat. Season with salt and pepper. Make at least 6 hours ahead, cover and refrigerate.

Roasted Vegetables and Rice

1 pound zucchini, diced
1 pound yellow squash, diced
1 large sweet onion, diced
1 large red bell pepper, diced
2 tablespoons olive oil
1 teaspoon seasoned salt
½ teaspoon freshly ground pepper
2 (8.5 oz.) packages of ready to serve brown and wild rice mix
½ cup chopped roasted salted almonds

Preheat oven to 450 degrees. Toss together first 7 ingredients until vegetables are well coated. Place vegetables in a single layer in a jelly roll pan. Bake for 20 minutes. Stir vegetables, and bake 20 more minutes or until slightly crisp and golden. Prepare rice according to package directions. Stir together rice, almonds, and hot vegetables.

Supper Time
FAVORITES

"For He satisfies the thirsty and fills the hungry with good things."

PSALM 107:9

Grandma Broz's Dressing

4 packages cornbread
4 slices of bread, cut into pieces
6 cups chicken broth
1 pound gizzards
2 stalks celery, chopped
½ onion, chopped
⅓ cup raisins
Salt and pepper to taste

Bake cornbread per directions on packages. While cornbread is baking, bring chicken broth to a boil in a large pot and add gizzards, celery and onions. Cook for 15 minutes or until gizzards are done. Remove gizzards and chop into pieces and discard grissel. Add cornbread, bread, chopped gizzards and raisins to chicken broth and vegetables. Place in casserole dish and bake covered at 325 degrees for 50 minutes. Add more chicken broth as needed to keep moist. Dressing can be placed in a turkey to bake instead of casserole dish.

Marlene's Macaroni and Cheese

1 ¼ cups uncooked macaroni
2 tablespoons butter, melted
2 tablespoons flour
¼ teaspoon salt
1 teaspoon Worcestershire sauce
1 teaspoon prepared mustard
⅛ teaspoon pepper
1 cup milk
2 cups extra sharp cheddar cheese
¼ cup cracker crumbs

Cook macaroni in boiling water until tender, drain and set aside. In medium bowl combine butter, flour, salt, Worcestershire sauce , mustard and pepper. Add milk, cheese, macaroni, and combine. Pour mixture into 2-quart baking dish and top with cracker crumbs. Bake at 350 degrees for 30 minutes or until golden brown.

King Ranch Chicken

1 large fryer, stewed, boned and cut in bite size pieces
1 large onion, chopped
1 large green pepper, chopped
10 (8 inch) flour tortillas
Stock from chicken
1 (10.5 oz.) can cream of mushroom soup
½ pound cheddar cheese, grated
1 teaspoon chili powder
Garlic salt to taste
1 (10.5 oz.) can cream of chicken soup
1 (10 oz.) can Ro-Tel tomatoes, crushed

Combine chicken, onion and green pepper. Layer alternately with tortillas, which have been dipped into hot chicken stock just long enough to soften, in a shallow 3-quart buttered casserole. Top with grated cheese and sprinkle with chili powder and garlic salt. Add in order: chicken soup, mushroom soup and tomatoes; bake in a 350 degrees oven for 30-45 minutes.

Baked Pasta

1 pound sweet Italian sausage
2 tablespoons olive oil
1 medium onion, chopped
3 cloves garlic, sliced
1 (28 oz.) can diced tomatoes
1 (15 oz.) can tomato sauce
2 tablespoons tomato paste
2 teaspoons sugar
¼ teaspoons salt
¼ teaspoon black pepper
1 (14.5 oz.) can basil and oregano diced tomatoes, drained
½ cup fresh basil leaves, chopped

1 (16 oz.) box ziti or other pasta of choice
1 (8 oz.) bag shredded mozzarella cheese
¼ cup grated Parmesan

Crumble 1 pound sweet Italian sausage in a 3-quart saucepan over medium heat. Cook 8 minutes, or until no longer pink. Remove from heat. Add onion to pot; cook 4 minutes. Add garlic and cook another minute. Stir in 28 oz. diced tomatoes and their juice. Stir in tomato sauce, tomato paste, sugar, salt and pepper. Simmer, stirring occasionally, for 20 minutes.

Remove pan from heat. Stir in sausage, basil and oregano diced tomatoes and basil. Bring a large pot of slightly salted water to boiling. Add pasta; boil 10 minutes. Drain and transfer to a large bowl. Add half the sauce to bowl with pasta. Stir to coat. Pour pasta mixture into prepared 9x13 greased dish. Top with remaining sauce then sprinkle with cheese.

Bake at 375 degrees for 20-25 minutes, until bubbly and lightly browned.

Black Bean and Chicken Enchilada Lasagna

2 (10 oz.) cans enchilada sauce
12 corn tortillas (6 inch)
2 cups coarsely shredded rotisserie chicken
1 small onion, chopped
1 (15 oz.) can black beans, rinsed and drained
3 (4 oz.) cans green chilies, drained and chopped
3 (12 oz.) cups Mexican cheese blend
2 medium ripe avocados
2 tablespoons sour cream
2 tablespoons lime juice
½ teaspoon salt
Chopped fresh tomatoes and cilantro

Preheat oven to 350 degrees. Spread ½ cup enchilada sauce into a greased 9x13 inch baking dish; top with four tortillas, 1 cup chicken, ¼ cup onion, ¼ cup beans, 1/3 cup green chilies and 1 cup cheese. Repeat layers. Drizzle with ½ cup enchilada sauce; top with the remaining tortillas, onions, beans, chilies, enchilada sauce and cheese.

Bake uncovered, 25-30 minutes until bubbly and cheese is melted. Let stand 10 minutes before serving.

Meanwhile, quarter, peel and pit one avocado; place in food processor. Add sour cream, lime juice and salt; process until smooth. Peel, pit and cut remaining avocado into small cubes.

Top lasagna with tomatoes, cilantro and cubed avocado. Serve with avocado sauce.

Sausage Pasta

¾ pound dried penne pasta
1 tablespoon olive oil
1 pound Italian sausage
(casing removed)
1 cup onion, finely chopped
4 cloves garlic, minced

1 (14.5 oz.) chicken broth
1 (14.5 oz.) can diced tomatoes, undrained
1 teaspoon dried basil
1 (10 oz.) package frozen chopped spinach, thawed
½ cup grated parmesan cheese

Cook pasta according to package instructions until al dente. Reserve ½ cup pasta water, then drain pasta. While pasta cooks, heat oil and sausage in a 12-inch skillet over medium high heat until sizzling. Reduce heat to medium and cook sausage, stirring and breaking up lumps with a spoon, until no longer pink, about 3 minutes. Add onion and garlic and cook until softened about5 minutes.

Add broth, tomatoes, and basil; bring to a boil over high heat. Reduce heat to medium high and cook, stirring occasionally, until slightly thickened, about 10 minutes. Add spinach, cover, and simmer over medium low heat, stirring once or twice, until spinach is tender, about 5 minutes.

Add pasta to skillet and cook 1 minute, stirring and adding enough reserved pasta water to keep moist. Remove from heat and sprinkle with cheese.

Lasagna

1 pound sweet Italian sausage
¾ pound lean ground beef
½ teaspoon minced onion
2 cloves garlic, crushed
1 (28 oz.) can crushed tomatoes
2 (6 oz.) cans tomato paste
2 (6.5 oz.) cans tomato sauce
½ cup water
2 tablespoons white sugar
1 ½ teaspoons dried basil leaves
½ teaspoon fennel seeds

1 teaspoon Italian seasoning
1 teaspoon salt
¼ teaspoon ground black pepper
4 tablespoons chopped fresh parsley
12 lasagna noodles
16 oz. ricotta cheese
1 egg
½ teaspoon salt
¾ pound mozzarella cheese
¾ cup grated parmesan cheese

In large skillet or Dutch oven, cook sausage, ground beef, onion and garlic over medium heat until well browned. Stir in crushed tomatoes, tomato paste, tomato sauce, and water. Season with sugar, basil, fennel seeds, Italian seasoning, 1 teaspoon salt, pepper and 2 tablespoons parsley. Simmer, covered, for about 1 ½ hours, stirring occasionally.

Bring a large pot of lightly salted water to a boil. Cook lasagna noodles in boiling water for 8 to 10 minutes. Drain noodles, and rinse with cold water. In a mixing bowl, combine ricotta cheese with egg, remaining parsley and ½ teaspoon salt.

Preheat oven to 375 degrees.

To assemble, spread 1 ½ cups of meat sauce in the bottom of a 9x13 inch baking dish. Arrange 6 noodles lengthwise over meat sauce. Spread with one half of the ricotta cheese mixture. Top with a third of mozzarella cheese. Spoon 1 ½ cups meat sauce over mozzarella and sprinkle with ¼ cup parmesan cheese.

Repeat layers, and top with remaining mozzarella and parmesan cheese. Cover with foil: to prevent sticking, spray foil with cooking spray. Bake in oven for 25 minutes. Remove foil and bake an additional 25 minutes. Cool for 15 minutes before serving.

Wholesome Enchilada

1 ¼ pounds lean ground turkey
1 small onion, chopped
1 teaspoon taco seasoning
½ teaspoon cumin
¼ teaspoon pepper
1 (8 oz.) cream cheese
1 (4 oz.) cup shredded Mexican cheese blend, divided
1 (15 oz.) can black beans, rinsed and drained
1 ½ cups frozen corn, thawed
1 (14.5 oz.) fire roasted diced tomatoes, drained
2 (4 oz.) cans green chilies, chopped
¼ cup salsa
14 whole wheat tortillas (8-inch), warmed
2 (10 oz.) cans enchilada sauce

Preheat oven to 375 degrees. In a nonstick skillet, cook turkey, onion and seasonings over medium heat 6-8 minutes or until turkey is cooked. Stir in cream cheese and ½ cup cheese until melted. Stir in beans, corn, tomatoes, chilies and salsa. Place ½ cup turkey mixture on each tortilla. Roll up and place in two 9x13 inch baking dishes coated with cooking spray, seam side down. Top with enchilada sauce; sprinkle with remaining cheese. Bake, uncovered, 15-20 minutes or until heated through.

This recipe makes enough for two meals or serves up to 14 people.

Chicken Pot Pie

1 cup peeled and diced potatoes
¾ cup sliced carrots
½ cup butter
⅔ cup onions, diced
1 ¼ teaspoons salt
½ teaspoon ground pepper
¼ teaspoon dried thyme
¼ teaspoon poultry seasoning

½ cup flour
3 cups shredded chicken
1 ½ cups chicken broth
1 cup milk
1 cup peas
2 pie crusts
1 egg white beaten together with 1 tablespoon water

Preheat oven to 425 degrees.

Place potatoes and carrots in small saucepan, cover with water and bring to boil 5-8 minutes to soften and then drain. Melt ½ cup butter in large saucepan. Add onion and saute for 2-3 minutes. Add salt, pepper, thyme, poultry seasoning and sprinkle flour on top and cook for 1 minute, stirring to evenly cook flour. Gradually whisk in chicken broth and then milk. Add potatoes and carrots and let simmer for a few minutes to thicken. Stir in chicken and peas.

Turn heat off.

Fit pie crust into bottom of a deep-dish pie plate. Pour filling into pie shell. Place second pie crust on top and trim excess. Brush egg white on top of the pot pie and use a knife to cut 4 slits to let steam escape.

Place on a baking sheet and place in oven and bake for 30 minutes or until golden brown.

Edna's Shrimp and Eggplant Casserole

1 large eggplant
1 large white onion, chopped
2 green onions, chopped
2 tablespoons bell pepper, chopped
2 stalks celery, chopped
1 teaspoon fresh parsley, chopped
2 tablespoons bacon drippings or vegetable oil
1 (10 ¾ oz.) can cream of mushroom soup
2 cups Pepperidge Farm herb stuffing
1 teaspoon seasoned salt
1 ½ cups grated cheese
2 pounds small fresh shrimp
Salt and pepper to taste

Peel eggplant, cut into 4 pieces, put in boiling salt water and cook about 15 minutes. Put bacon drippings or oil in a skillet and saute onions, bell pepper, celery and parsley until vegetables are tender. Drain eggplant and add to skillet with vegetables. Chop eggplant with wooden spoon (to prevent eggplant from turning dark).

Mix in raw shrimp, herb stuffing, soup and sprinkle with seasoned salt. Mix well, using light strokes. If too thick add ½ soup can of water. Pour into 9x13 dish, cover, and bake at 325 degrees for 30 minutes or until shrimp are pink in color. Sprinkle cheese over top, cover and bake 10 minutes or until cheese is melted.

Spaghetti Sauce

1 pound Italian sausage
½ pound ground beef
½ cup chopped onion
2 cloves garlic, chopped
1 (28 oz.) can crushed tomatoes
2 (6 oz.) cans tomato paste
2 (6 oz.) cans tomato sauce
½ cup water
2 tablespoons sugar
1 ½ teaspoon dried basil
½ teaspoon fennel seed
1 teaspoon Italian seasoning
½ teaspoon salt
¼ teaspoon pepper
3 tablespoons fresh parsley

Cook sausage, beef, onion and garlic until well browned; drain fat. Stir in crushed tomatoes, tomato paste, tomato sauce, and water. Mix in sugar and season with basil, fennel seed, Italian seasoning, salt, pepper and parsley. Reduce heat to low, cover and simmer for 1 ½ hours.

Breakfast Casserole

1 pound sausage
6 medium or large eggs
2 cups milk
1 teaspoon salt
1 teaspoon dry mustard
6 slices bread, buttered, without crust
½ grated cheese
1 (4 oz.) can sliced mushrooms

Brown sausage, drain and cool. Beat eggs and milk, add salt and dry mustard. Put bread pieces in bottom of 9x13 greased dish. Sprinkle browned sausage, add cheese and egg mixture. Let stand overnight in refrigerator. Bake uncovered at 350 degrees for 30 minutes.

Chicken and Black Bean Chimichangas

1 pound shredded chicken
1 (15 oz.) can black beans, drained & rinsed
1 (4 oz.) can mild chopped green chilies
¼ cup salsa verde
½ teaspoon salt

¼ teaspoon pepper
¼ cup chopped fresh cilantro
8 flour tortillas (6-8 inch)
1 cup shredded Monterey Jack cheese
⅓ cup Canola oil

Stir together first 7 ingredients in a large bowl. Divide chicken mixture among tortillas, placing mixture just below center of each tortilla. Sprinkle with cheese. Fold sides of tortilla over filling, and roll up. Fry chimichangas in hot oil in a large skillet over medium heat 3 to 4 minutes on each side or until browned and crispy. Drain on paper towels. Serve with desired toppings.

SLOWER
than molasses...

"For no good tree bears
bad fruit, nor again
does a bad tree
bear good fruit."

LUKE 6:43

Roast Beef and Gravy

1 boneless beef chuck roast (3 pounds)
2 (10 ¾ oz.) cans cream of mushroom soup
⅓ cup beef broth
1 envelope onion soup mix

Cut roast in half; place in a 3-quart slow cooker. In a large bowl, combine remaining ingredients; pour over roast. Cover and cook on low for 8-9 hours or until meat is tender.

Garlic Chicken

1 teaspoon salt
1 teaspoon paprika
½ teaspoon pepper
1 teaspoon olive oil
3 ½ pound cut up frying chicken
1 large onion, sliced
4-5 cloves garlic, chopped

In small bowl, mix salt, paprika, pepper and oil for form paste; spread evenly over each piece of chicken.

In 5 to 6 quart slow cooker, place onion slices. Arrange chicken over onion. Place chopped garlic over and around chicken.

Cover; cook on low setting 7 to 8 hours.

Serve with Roasted Vegetables and Rice.

Makes 6 servings.

Creamy Chicken

6 skinned and boned chicken breasts (about 2 ½ lbs.)
2 teaspoons seasoned salt
2 tablespoons canola oil
1 (10 ¾ oz.) can cream of mushroom soup
1 (8 oz.) package cream cheese
½ cup dry white wine
1 (0.7 oz.) envelope Italian dressing mix
1 (8 oz.) package sliced fresh mushrooms

Sprinkle chicken with seasoned salt. Cook chicken, in batches, in hot oil in a large skillet over medium heat 2 to 3 minutes on each side or just until browned. Transfer chicken to a 5 quart slow cooker, reserving drippings in skillet.

Add soup, cream cheese, white wine, and Italian dressing mix to hot drippings in skillet. Cook over medium heat, stirring constantly, 2 to 3 minutes or until cheese is melted and mixture is smooth.

Arrange mushrooms over chicken in slow cooker. Spoon soup mixture over mushrooms.

Cover and cook on low 4 hours. Stir well before serving.

Serve with fresh green beans.

Chicken Tortilla Soup

1 pound shredded, cooked chicken
1 (15 oz.) can diced tomatoes
1 (10 oz.) can enchilada sauce
1 medium onion, chopped
1 (4 oz.) can chopped green chilies
2 cloves garlic, minced
2 cups water
1 (14.5 oz.) can chicken broth
1 teaspoon cumin
1 teaspoon chili powder
1 teaspoon salt
¼ teaspoon black pepper
1 bay leaf
1 (10 oz.) package frozen corn
1 tablespoon chopped cilantro

Place chicken, tomatoes, enchilada sauce, onion, green chilies, and garlic into slow cooker. Pour in water and chicken broth, and season with cumin, chili powder, salt, pepper, and bay leaf. Stir in corn and cilantro. Cover, and cook on low setting for 6 to 8 hours or on high for 3 to 4 hours. Serve with chips and cheese for toppings.

Beef Vegetable Soup

1 pound boneless beef chuck roast, cut into bite-size pieces
3 medium carrots, cut into ½ inch thick slices
2 small potatoes, cut into ½ inch cubes
1 medium onion, chopped
½ teaspoon salt
½ teaspoon dried thyme
1 bay leaf
2 cans (14.5 oz.) diced tomatoes
1 cup water
1 can (14.5 oz.) beef broth
2 beef bouillon cubes
½ cup frozen peas

In 3 ½ or 4-quart slow cooker, combine beef, carrots, potatoes and onion. Sprinkle with salt and thyme. Add bay leaf. Add tomatoes with their juices, water beef broth and bouillon cubes. Cover slow cooker; cook on low heat setting for 8 to 10 hours or on high heat setting for 4 to 5 hours. Remove and discard bay leaf. Stir in frozen peas. Garnish with parsley if desired.

Makes 4 servings.

Hearty Beef Chili

1 ½ pounds lean ground beef
1 can (16 oz.) tomato sauce
1 can (15 oz.) dark red kidney beans, rinsed
1 can (15 oz.) light red kidney beans, rinsed
1 ½ cups thick and chunky mild salsa
1 cup frozen corn, thawed and drained
1 onion, chopped
2 tablespoons chili powder
1 cup Mexican style finely shredded four cheeses

Brown meat; drain. Add to slow cooker with remaining ingredients except cheese; stir. Cover with lid. Cook on low 5 to 6 hours or high for 3 to 4 hours. Stir before serving. Serve topped with cheese and onions, if desired.

Healthy Turkey Chili

2 tablespoons oil
1 pound ground turkey
1 medium onion, chopped
1 (15 oz.) can black beans, undrained
1 (15 oz.) can pinto beans, undrained
1 (15 oz.) can diced tomatoes, undrained
1 (11 oz.) can whole kernel corn, undrained
1 (1 oz.) package dry ranch dressing mix
1 (1 ¼ oz.) package taco seasoning (spicy if desired)

Heat oil in saucepan over medium heat. Heat onion, stirring occasionally, until browned, 8 to 9 minutes. Add turkey and cook, breaking up with a wooden spoon, until cooked through, 4 to 5 minutes. Add remaining ingredients and cook on low setting for 3 to 4 hours.

Pulled Pork Sandwiches

3 pound pork shoulder
10 oz. Root beer
Barbeque Sauce of liking (I use Sweet Baby Ray's)

Place pork shoulder in slow cooker and add Root beer. Cook low for 6-7 hours or high for 4-5 hours. Remove meat and cool, pull apart and shred with fork or hands. Add sauce to meat and toss to coat, adding more sauce as needed. Serve on buns with coleslaw.

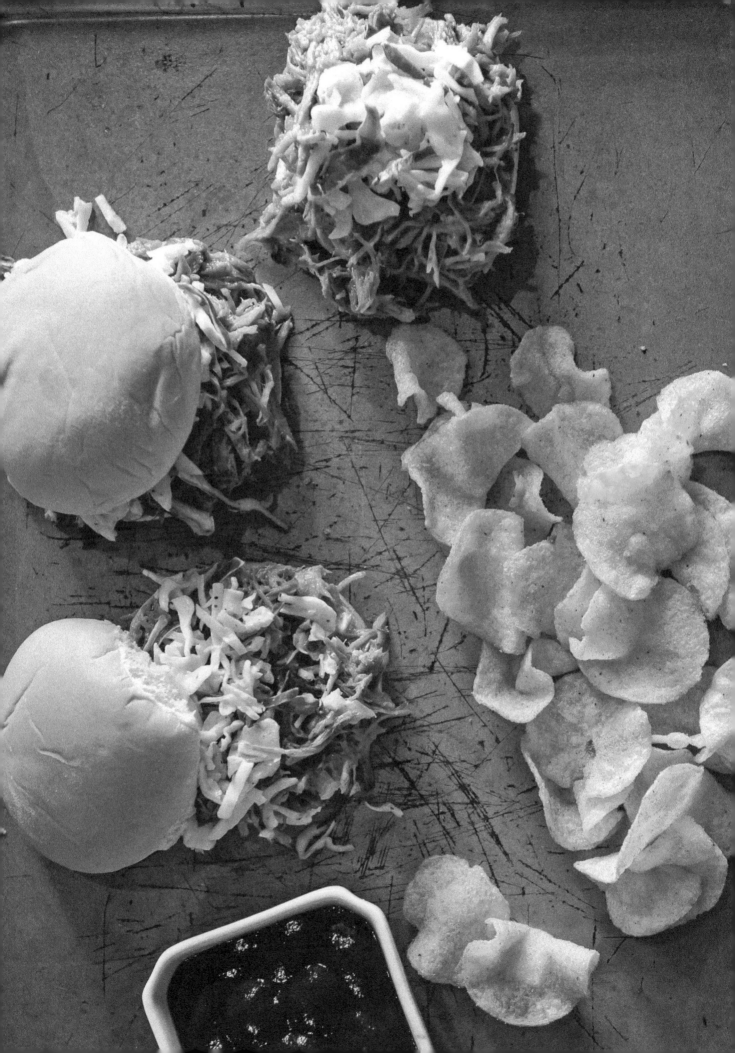

WHAT
Nots

" Oh, taste and see
that the Lord is good!
Blessed is the man
who takes refuge
in Him."

PSALM 34:8

Mom's Cereal Snack

⅓ cup butter, melted
3 teaspoons seasoned salt
5 teaspoons Worcestershire sauce
8-9 cups Crispix cereal

Preheat oven to 250 degrees. Mix butter, salt and Worcestershire sauce. Mix with cereal in a large bowl. Spray 9x13 baking pan and pour mixture evenly onto pan. Bake 45 minutes, stirring every 15 minutes.

Grandma Broz's Barbecue Sauce

24 oz. ketchup
½ stick butter
½ cup water
1 cup sugar
2 lemons, quartered
3 tablespoons white vinegar
1 medium onion, finely chopped
1 teaspoon Worcestershire sauce
1 teaspoon salt
¼ teaspoon black pepper
¼ teaspoon chili powder

Cook all ingredients until medium thick. Discard lemons before storing sauce.

Bircher Muesli

½ cup raisins
½ cup old fashioned oats
1 ½ cups quick oats
¼ cup brown sugar
½ teaspoon cinnamon
2 cups milk
Fresh Fruit

Mix all ingredients except fruit and refrigerate overnight. Add more milk
if too thick. Serve with any fresh fruit.

Grandma Broz's Noodles

12 brown eggs plus 4 more egg yolks
2 teaspoons salt
6-8 cups flour

Beat eggs with mixer until light and fluffy. Add salt and 6 cups flour. Add more flour until it is no longer sticky. Knead until dough is not sticking to your hands and roll into long log and cut into approximately 9 sections. Sprinkle each with a little flour and cover with wax paper while you take out each one and roll out into small circles about ¼ inch. Lay out rolled out circles onto brown paper sacks to dry, turning every 30 minutes.

It will take around 6 hours to dry enough to cut with a knife. When ready, cut with a knife into long strips and make noodles approximately 2 inches in length. After all noodles are cut, lay out on brown paper sacks to continue to dry. Place in baggies and freeze until ready to use.

Icebox Pickles

6 cups water
1 ½ cups vinegar
⅓ cup pickling salt

12 dried red peppers
12 cloves garlic
Dill, one bunch
8 grape leaves
1 onion, sliced
Pickling cucumbers
4 quart jars

Boil first 3 ingredients. For each jar, arrange dill on the bottom of jar, add cucumbers, 3 dried red peppers, 3 cloves garlic, 2 grape leaves and a few sliced onions. Fill jar with boiling brine and end with dill on top. Seal and place in refrigerator, ready in 2 weeks. Makes 4 quarts.

Barkin'
UP THE WRONG TREE

"A righteous man
has regard for
the life of his animal."
PROVERBS 12:10

Mom's Dog Treats

1 cup canned pumpkin
½ cup peanut butter
2 eggs
½ cup vegetable oil
2 ½ cups flour
1 teaspoon baking soda

Mix all ingredients and roll out and use cookie cutter to cut out dog bone shapes. Bake at 350 degrees for 20-25 minutes. Drizzle with bacon grease combined with peanut butter.

If your dog is sensitive to wheat, rice flour can be substituted for flour.

personal testimony

It has taken me my whole life to get to a place of rest, quietness and stillness and to listen to God's voice to know and decipher the choices in life that lead to balance we all so desperately need. I guess you want to know now that, since I have found balance and rest to hear God's word, my life is perfect? Well no, I can't say that, and for the most part, no one on earth will ever get to that place of perfection, but we can stand firm and have peace and joy in our life amidst the chaos. Even Jesus experienced pressure and stress from all the things He was doing. In Mark 1:21-34 it tells of all the things He did, but look at Mark 1:35; the one thing Jesus did that was crucial to his life and the impact He made on others was finding solitude and quiet to pray and to gain peace, rest and strength.

It seems my relationships with others, including my spouse, were not what they should be and, over the years, I grew to understand that, no, it wasn't everyone else but it was me. I finally found a counselor that a friend of mine was going to, and at first, I was happy that she was finally getting help, and then God nudged me and said, "You should go too." I was handling my life just fine, and so I thought. I began counseling with this sweet Christian lady, and months led into years, and I was steady in seeking her counsel each week. The love of Jesus she shared with me brought me to a place that I knew that God was revealing himself to me through her. I found that the balance in my life was off, and that I desperately needed to turn things around so that I could have peace and joy in my life. Not a perfect life, but a life filled with Jesus.

I began to understand that I needed Jesus more than ever in my life and began studying His word and making time for devotion with Him. After that, I knew I needed to make my husband next in my life, to praise him and lift him up and cherish what God had given me. The hard part came with letting go of so much control in my life, whether with myself, my husband, or my children. I had to let go of a failed marriage and relationships that were hurting my spirit, and to say God respects me and He does not want others continually hurting me. This began a healing process where I respected myself and used God's power to work through me.

Saying I'm a Christian is not saying I'm perfect, it is actually saying I know I'm not perfect and I need help each day to become more like Christ. We first admit that we are lost and have sinned and come short of the glory of God. Then we believe that we need God and are in need of a Savior. We know that we are sinners and want to turn away from our sins. We receive Christ as our Savior.

John 3:16 says **"For God so loved the world, that He gave His only begotten Son, that whosoever believeth in Him should not perish, but have everlasting life"**.

about me

I grew up on a small farm in Texas. The only thing I could ever remember wanting more in life was a horse. I prayed for a horse every day, and finally my dreams came true to the tune of an eighteen-year-old Appaloosa named Rojo. I never got to compete, but spent many a day riding bare back with flip-flops on to see my grandparents. The good ol' days, when summers were spent mostly outdoors fishing, picking up rocks, riding bikes, playing with dogs and cats, and riding a horse.

After high school, I got married and, a few years later, started a family. I have a daughter and a son. My daughter is currently at Texas A&M University (Whoop!), working on her degree to become a veterinarian. My son is a senior in high school and is currently studying to become a pilot. Both have been active in 4-H, FFA, raising and showing animals, fishing, hunting, riding horses, and countless other activities. They both love Jesus, and for that, I am most blessed. "If God is all you have, you have all you need" (John 14:8).

After years of marriage, I found myself divorced and raising two children. It is true that no one lives a perfect life, but I did find the love of my life and have been happily married for six years. I am actively enjoying barrel racing and also compete in mounted shooting competitions with my husband. We share our love of horses together. We also love spending time with family, and combined, we have five children, two daughters-in-law, two sons-in-law, four granddaughters and one grandson. But most importantly, we both love the Lord and make it a priority to seek His will for our lives and our marriage.

I have a love and passion for cooking and baking. I am grateful to have many influences in my life to help me learn. God has given me ambition and abilities to do all that I strive to be. I have felt called to write and share with others what God has blessed my life with, and I am thankful to share it through this cookbook.

May He give you the desire of your heart and make all your plans succeed. Psalm 20:4

Index

Thank Yous

God for giving me this opportunity
Brion for your love and support
Family and Friends for participating and encouragement

Photo Shoot Locations

McCall's Antiques, Caldwell, Texas
Still Waters Ranch, Burton, Texas
Evonne and Roger Schulz, Fayetteville, Texas
Bessie Broz, Bleiblerville, Texas
St. John's Lutheran Church, New Wehdem, Texas
Lydia's House, Brenham, Texas
Darcee and Hunter Andras, Brenham, Texas
Bluebird Off The Square, Brenham, Texas
Naples, Maine

Art Work and Calligraphy

Darcee Andras

Photographers

Uncle Tio Photography, Brenham, Texas
Fields of Heather Photography, Brenham, Texas
Ashleigh London Photography, Naples, Maine

Desktop Publishing

Diane Horstman www.BusyBeeInspirations.com

For more information: www.simplysouthernbooks.com

*May the Lord now show you kindness and
faithfulness, and I too will show you the same
favor because you have done this.*
Samuel 2:6

CPSIA information can be obtained
at www.ICGtesting.com
Printed in the USA
LVHW051055220219
608390LV00001B/9/P